Collins

Primary Social Studies for Antigua and Barbuda

STUDENT'S BOOK
Kindergarten

Anthea S Thomas

William Collins' dream of knowledge for all began with the publication of his first book in 1819. A self-educated mill worker, he not only enriched millions of lives, but also founded a flourishing publishing house.

Today, staying true to this spirit, Collins books are packed with inspiration, innovation and practical expertise. They place you at the centre of a world of possibility and give you exactly what you need to explore it.

Collins. Freedom to teach.

Published by Collins
An imprint of HarperCollins*Publishers*
The News Building, 1 London Bridge Street,
London SE1 9GF

HarperCollins*Publishers*
Macken House, 39/40 Mayor Street Upper,
Dublin 1, D01 C9W8, Ireland

Browse the complete Collins Caribbean catalogue at
www.collins.co.uk/caribbeanschools

Author: Anthea S. Thomas
Reviewer: Rochelle Richards
Publisher: Elaine Higgleton
Senior editor: Lucy Cooper
Development editor: Fiona MacGregor
Cover designers: Kevin Robbins and Gordon MacGilp
Artwork and cover image: Zavian Archibald
Typesetter: Jouve, India
Printed in the UK using 100% Renewable Electricity at CPI Group (UK) Ltd

Collins would like to thank the following teachers who read and reviewed the materials in proof and gave valuable feedback:

Philip Lloyd, Curriculum Officer for Social Studies
Neilson Duberry
Francille Francis
Jacqueline Jackson
Vill Peters
Janice Walbrook

Acknowledgements
The Publishers wish to thank the following for permission to reproduce photographs. Every effort has been made to trace copyright holders and to obtain their permission for the use of copyright materials. The Publishers will gladly receive any information enabling them to rectify any error or omission at the first opportunity.

Image acknowledgements
Photogenesis Imaging, Antigua & Barbuda: pages 20 tl, br, bl; 36 tr, bl,br; 43; 44; 45; 54br; 55 tl,tr,br; 58; 59;62; 63 bm, br; 70; 71; pages 71 + 72: APUA logo © APUA; ABS logo © ABS; Flow logo © Flow; Digicel logo © Digicel - all provided by Photogenesis Imaging, Antigua & Barbuda.
Alamy: pages 26r Robert Fried; 32tl Image Broker (Florian Kopp); 32br Grant Rooney
Shutterstock: page 42t, Ervin Monn.
All other images from Shutterstock.
t=top, m=middle, b=bottom, r=right, l=left

Contents

Topic 1: About me

Hello! My name is Shemika and this is my brother, Jaden.

We live in a town in Antigua with our family.

These are our friends who live next door. They are from Guyana.

Kayla and Laurisa are girls. Omar is a boy. We like our neighbours.

We play and sing songs. Do you know this song?

Head, shoulders,
knees and toes
knees and toes
Head, shoulders,
knees and toes
knees and toes
And eyes and ears
and mouth and nose
Head, shoulders,
knees and toes
knees and toes.

Sing with us!

I am short.   Laurisa has   Kayla has
              curly hair.   long hair.

Jaden is tall.   Omar has a wheelchair.

We are all different, but we are
all the same.

It is my birthday. I draw an invitation.

Palm Tree Lane,
Ottos Village,
St John's Parish

Come to my birthday party
On 12th April 2022
At Avec Amour
Phone to say yes or no:
1-268-773-1912

My friends are coming. We will have cake. It's a party!

April

S	M	T	W	T	F	S
					1	2
3	4	5	6	7	8	9
10	11	12	13	14	15	16
17	18	19				

We dance and sing and have fun.

Then we help tidy up.
It was a good day.

Today we go and help Grandma.
I can be kind.

I can be helpful.

I respect my elders.

Jaden makes tea, while I sweep Grandma's yard.

Keeping clean and healthy

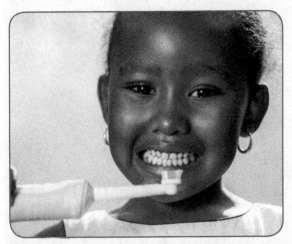

I brush my teeth.

I comb my hair.

I wash my face.

I wash the clothes.

I exercise.

I eat healthy food.

I wash my hands.

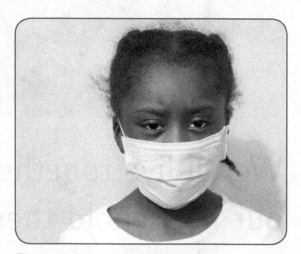

I wear a mask.

Topic 2: One happy family

Hello! We are the Thomas family.

We all live together in Barbuda. In our household there is mom, dad, grandma, grandpa, my sister Tiana, and me, Kairo.

We are a big family. Our kind of family is called an extended family, because there is more than a mother and father with their children.

Auntie Dawn is also visiting us at the moment, with her baby K'myah. This is a single parent family.

You already know my cousins Shemika and Jaden. Look, here is a photograph of them with Uncle Paul and Auntie Rose.

They are a small family. This kind of family, with a mom and dad and children, is called a nuclear family.

Here is a poem about families.

Families share
With one another
Mother, father,
Sister, brother.

Families can be
Big or small
As long as there
Is love for all.

Dad and mom are the leaders of our family. But we all have jobs to do.

Dad is a fisherman.

Mom is the secretary at the school.

My job is washing the dishes.

Tiana sweeps the yard.

What are our basic needs?

food

work

protection

shelter

health

clothing

...but, most of all, love.

Where in the wide, wide world are we?

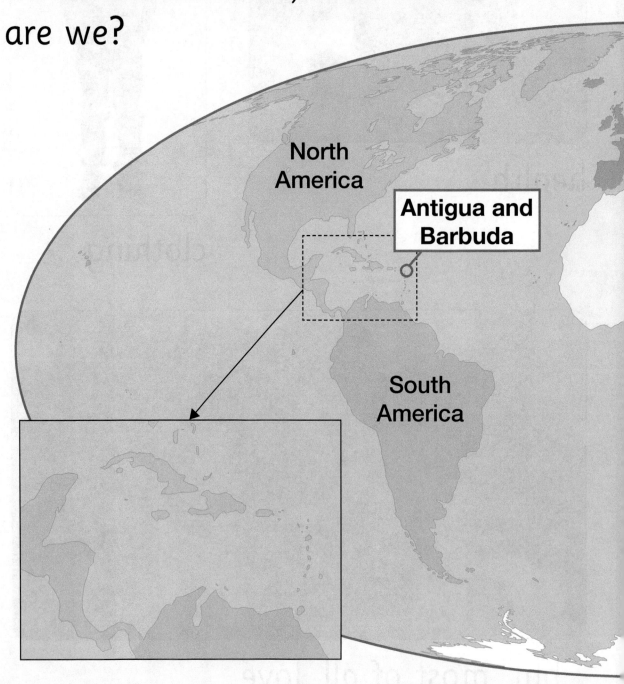

North America

Antigua and Barbuda

South America

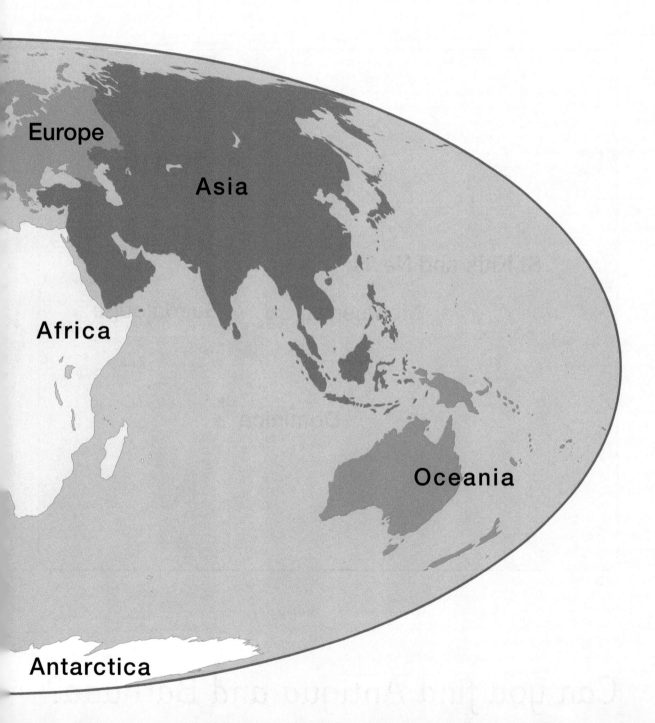

This is a map of our near neighbours in the Caribbean.

St Kitts and Nevis

Antigua and Barbuda

Montserrat

Guadaloupe

Dominica

Can you find Antigua and Barbuda?

Where do you live?

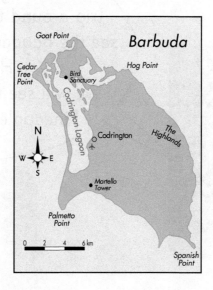

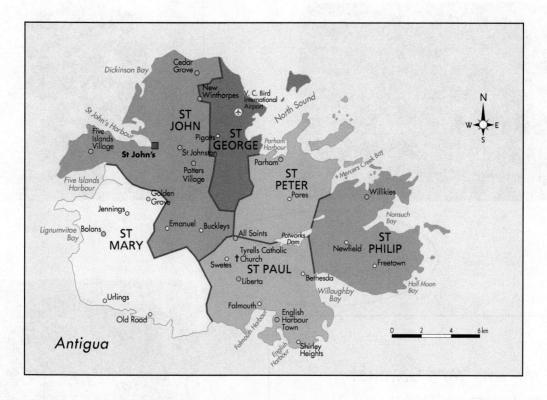

Find your parish and your nearest town on the map.

A school trip

We are going on a field trip around the island. We will see the dagger log tree at English Harbour.
We will see the Antigua Black Pineapple at Cades Bay.

Here is the letter from the school.

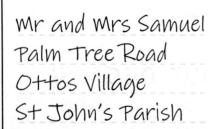

Mr and Mrs Samuel
Palm Tree Road
Ottos Village
St John's Parish

These are some of our national symbols.

Hawksbill turtle

Fallow deer

Wow

We live in a beautiful place.

Frigate bird

At the end of our school trip, we sing the National Anthem.

Fair Antigua and Barbuda
We thy sons and daughters stand
Strong and firm in peace or danger,
To safeguard our native land.
We commit ourselves to building
A true nation, brave and free!
Ever striving, ever seeking,
Dwell in love and unity.

Raise the standard! Raise it boldly!
Answer now to duty's call
To the service of your country,
Sparing nothing giving all;
Gird your loins and join the battle
'Gainst fear, hate and poverty
Each endeavoring, all achieving,
Live in peace where man is free!

God of nations, let thy blessings
Fall upon this land of ours
Rain and sunshine ever sending
Fill her fields with crops and flowers.
We her children do implore Thee:
Give us strength, faith, loyalty
Never failing, all enduring
To defend her liberty.

Topic 4: Watch out, be careful!

At home we have a safety rhyme.

Pick up your toys
Be good girls and boys
Don't play with fire
Put down that wire.

In Kairo and Tiana's house they have different rules.

Don't swing on the gate
Or fall out of a tree
Look out for the thorns
Be safe, you and me.

Safety at school

Rules keep us safe. They protect us from danger.

Classroom Rules

Raise your hands to speak.

Do not litter.

Walk to the left of the hall.

Respect each other.

Rules teach us to share, care and be fair. We must obey the rules.

Safety on the road

We obey the rules of the road.

Cross at the pedestrian crossing.
Don't talk to strangers.

Who keeps us safe?

doctor

police officer

fire fighter

crossing guard

What can go wrong?

You could hurt yourself.
You could hurt others.
Be kind and obey the rules.

Topic 5: At school

Kairo and Tiana go to Grove Primary School.
Can you find it on the map?

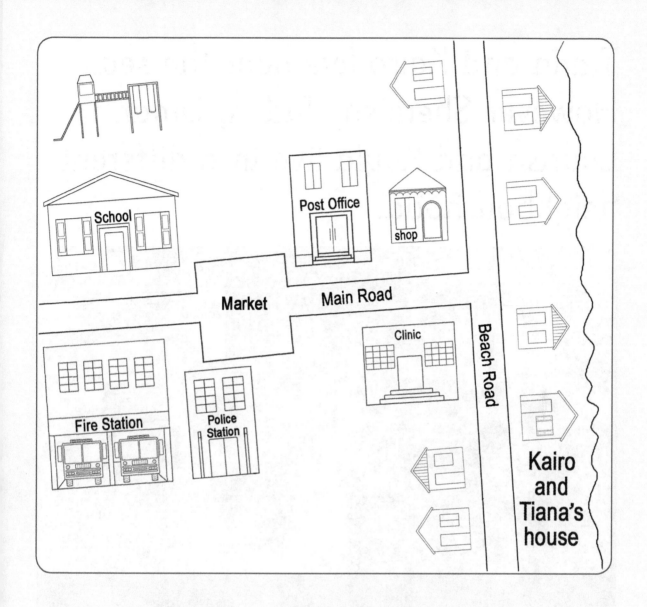

Go along Beach Road. Turn left into Main Road. Pass the shop and the post office. Walk through the market. The school is on the right, after the market.

Tiana and Kairo live near the sea. However Shemika, Jaden, Omar, Laurisa and Kayla live in a different neighbourhood.

They go to Mill Primary School. Can you find it on the map?

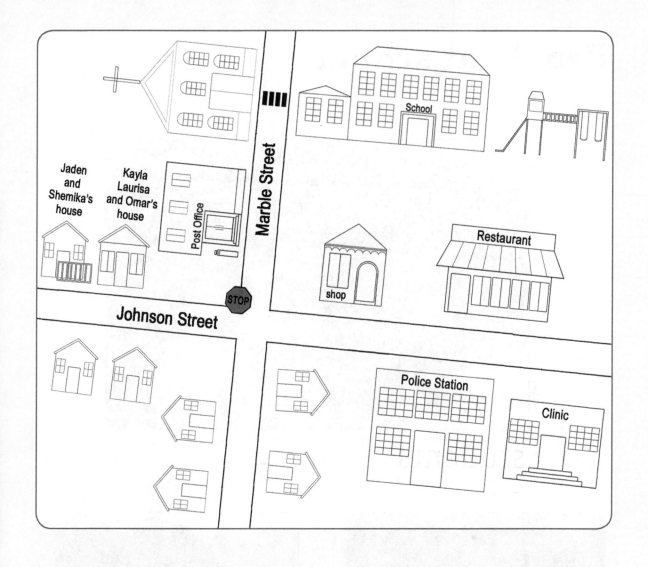

Go along Johnson Street until you come to the STOP sign. Turn left. Go down Marble Street. Pass the post office and the church. Cross the road at the pedestrian crossing. You are at school.

People at school

students

teacher

principal

secretary

cleaner

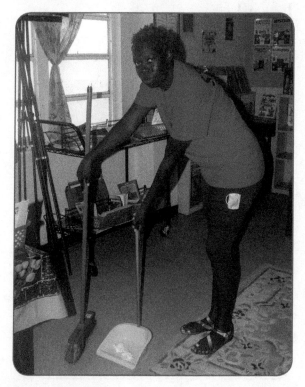

janitor

groundsman

Places at school

classroom

bathroom

lunchroom

office

library

playground

our school

A rhyme about school

Wake up, get up
It's a lovely day

We're off to school
To learn and play

Kayla, what is your school's motto?

A sound education makes an intelligent nation.

That's a good one. Ours is Accept No Limits.

1. Be respectful to others.
2. Be responsible for your own actions.
3. Keep hands and feet to self.
4. Give others their privacy.
5. Play with children your own size.

These are our school's expectations.

Ours are almost the same.

Topic 6: My Community

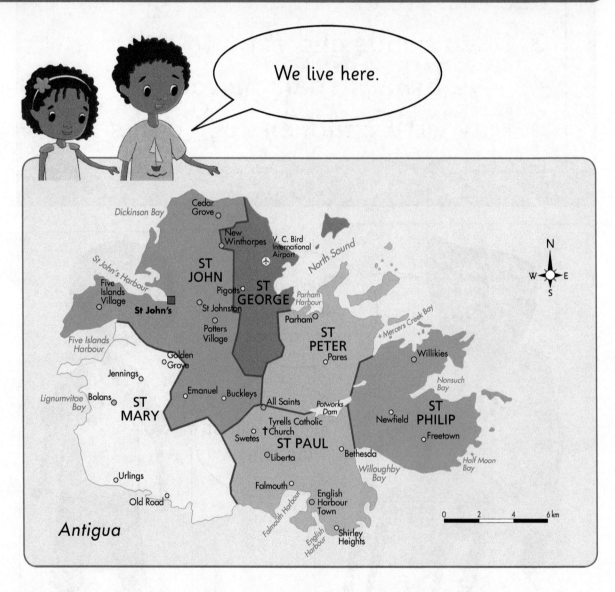

We live here.

Shemika and Jaden live
in St John's Parish.

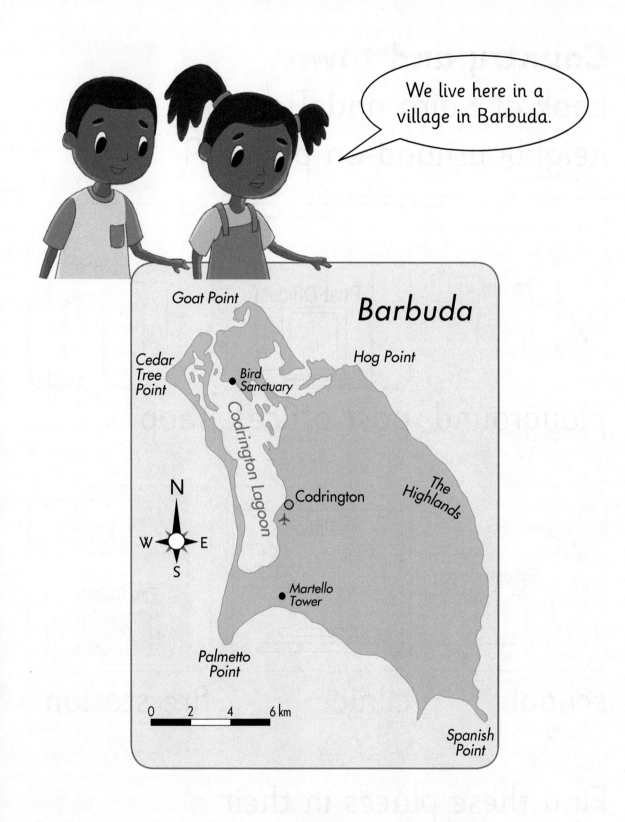

This is Kairo and Tiana's community.

Country and town

Look at Kairo and Tiana's neighbourhood on page 39.

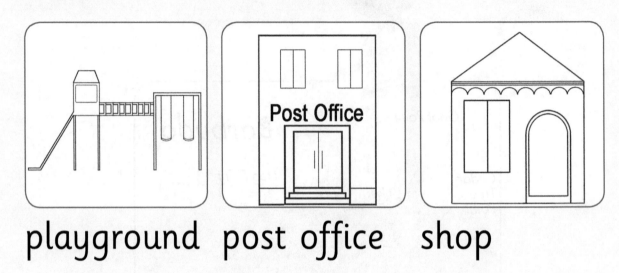

playground   post office   shop

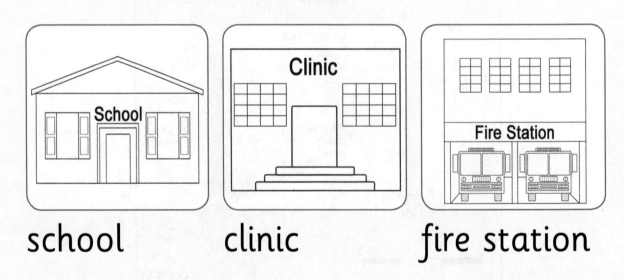

school   clinic   fire station

Find these places in their neighbourhood.

Look at Shemika and Jaden's neighbourhood on page 41.

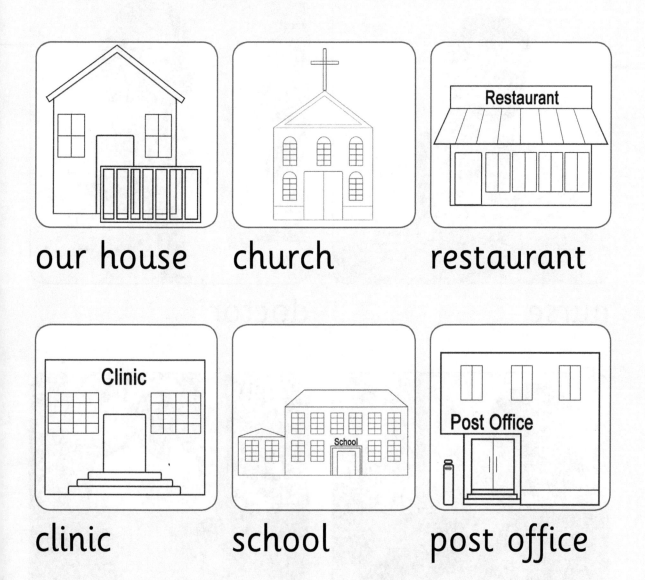

our house   church   restaurant

clinic   school   post office

Find these places in their neighbourhood.

Community workers

nurse

doctor

dentist

police officer

fire fighter

postwoman

shopkeeper

barber

Topic 7: Transportation

We walk to school.

Omar rolls in his wheelchair.

My dad drives to work.

Kayla and Laurisa ride their bicycles.

Look at all the different forms of transport.

Dad takes the fish to market in his truck. The car carries plantain and other vegetables.

Dad gives Mom a lift on shopping days. Those bags are heavy!

Our transport centres and workers

VC Bird International Airport

West Bus Station

St John's Harbour

pilot

bus driver

captain

Topic 8: Communication

Kairo and Tiana sing a welcome song.

Mom is staying at home while Shemika and Jaden visit their cousins. She says goodbye.

In Barbuda, the boys go fishing.

Shemika sends mom a text.
Mom sends Shemika an email.

On the last night, they watch
TV together.

Home tomorrow!

Our communication centres

Post Office

APUA

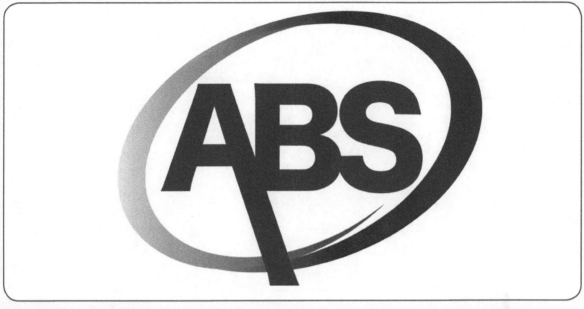

ABS TV

Flow

Digicel